SMART COOKIE KID

For 3 - 4 year olds

Mary Khalil
Baha Kodir

PREFACE

This developmental workbook features a variety of engaging exercises designed to enhance your child's attention, concentration, multiple intelligences, visual memory, motor skills, critical thinking, learning abilities, problem-solving, creativity, and more. For optimal results, we recommend that children complete these activities sequentially and regularly, with the guidance of an adult. Every exercise in this entertaining and attention-boosting book is accompanied by clear instructions. There is no specific time limit for each exercise. What's most important is that your child enjoys focusing their attention while solving problems and learning new skills.

If your child ever finds the instructions confusing during an activity, it's important to clarify those confusions with a simple and relatable explanation or by providing an example. Positive verbal encouragement is a great way to motivate your child when they successfully complete the exercises. For instance, you can say, 'You're doing an amazing job!' or 'You're incredibly awesome!'

The book features delightful illustrations created with care and expertise, specifically tailored to captivate children's imaginations. These works of gentle art are the result of the talents of professional artists.

In addition, we've included entertaining game pages to provide parents with quality bonding time at home with their children. These fun games are sure to create memorable moments and foster a strong connection between you and your little ones.

Match the uncolored shapes of the balls.

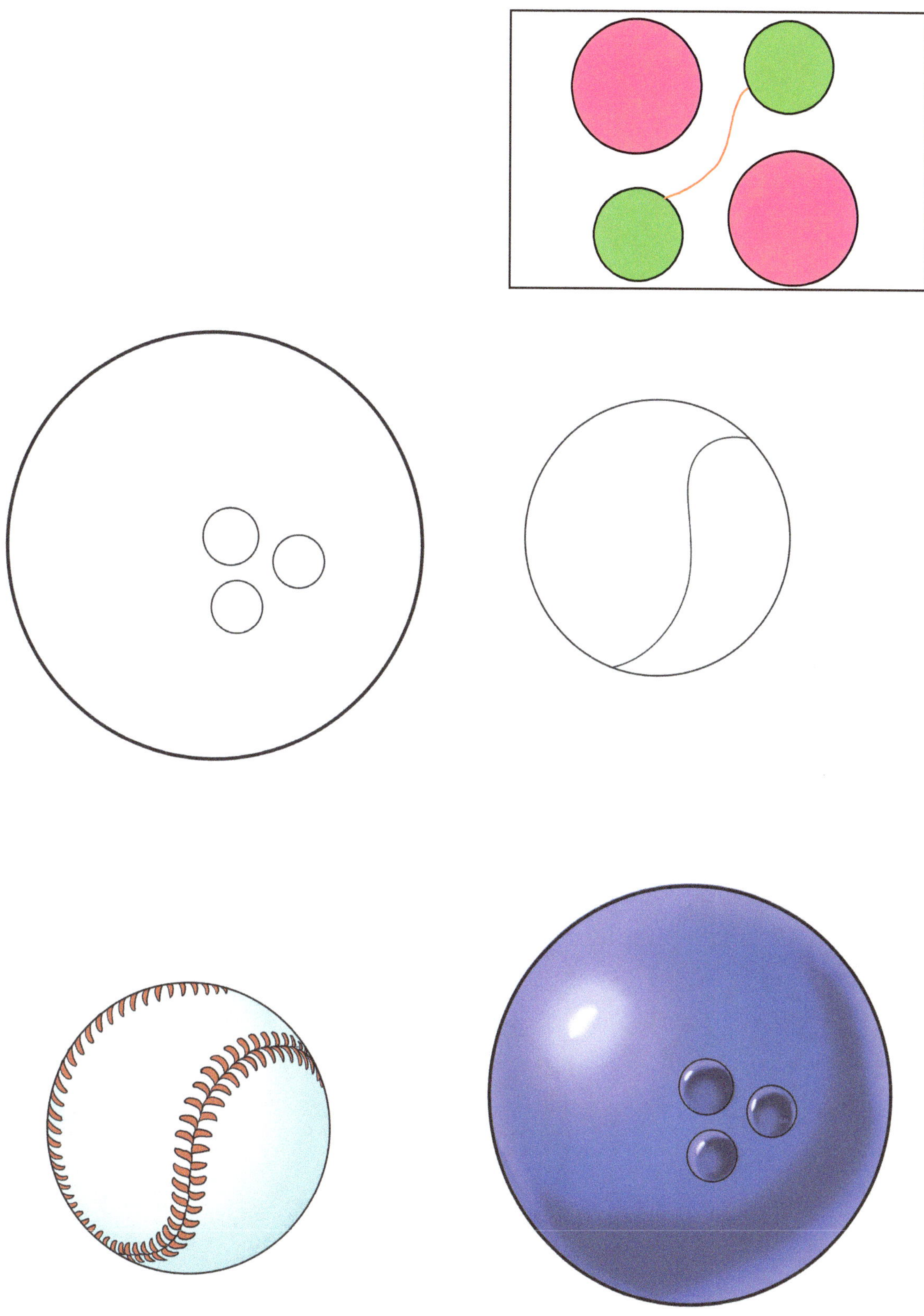

Find smiling faces.

Which one should be painted blue?

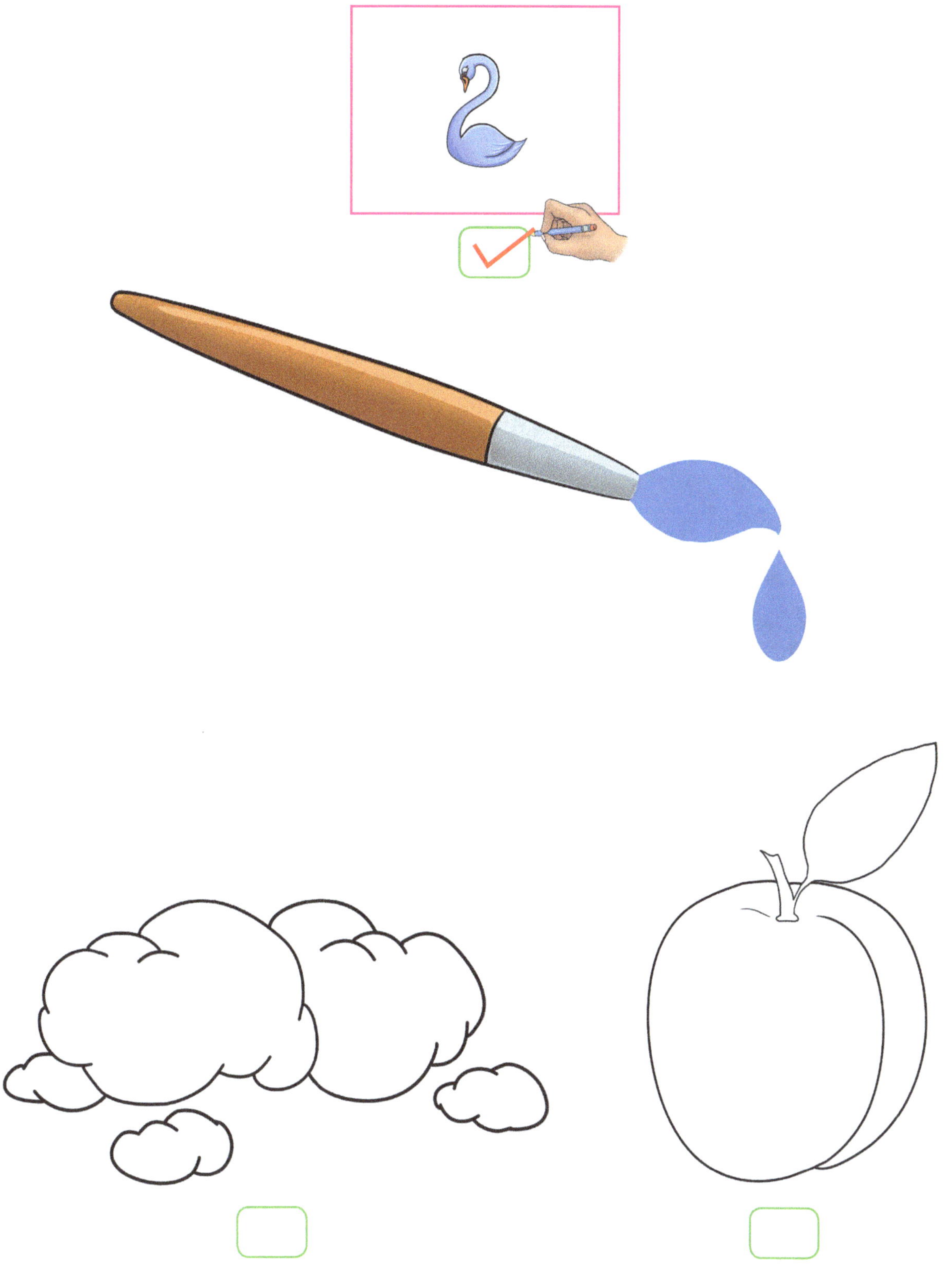

Which one do we taste?

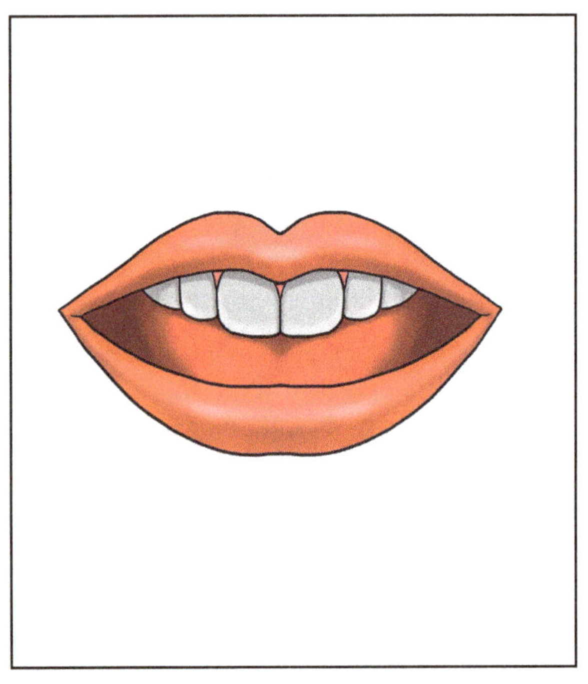

Complete the circle drawing the other half.

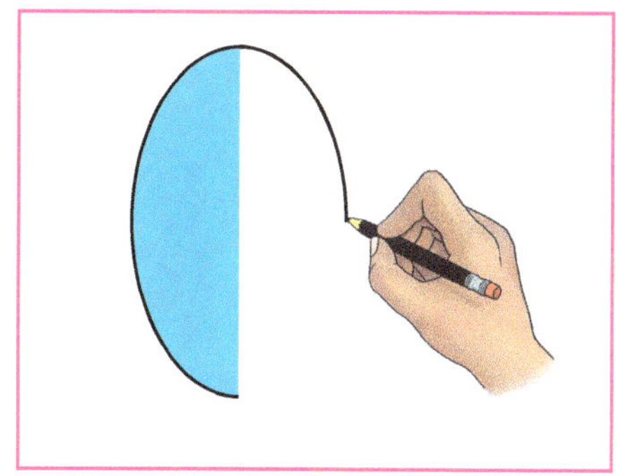

Find four differences between two piggies.

Draw more black dots on the ladybug.

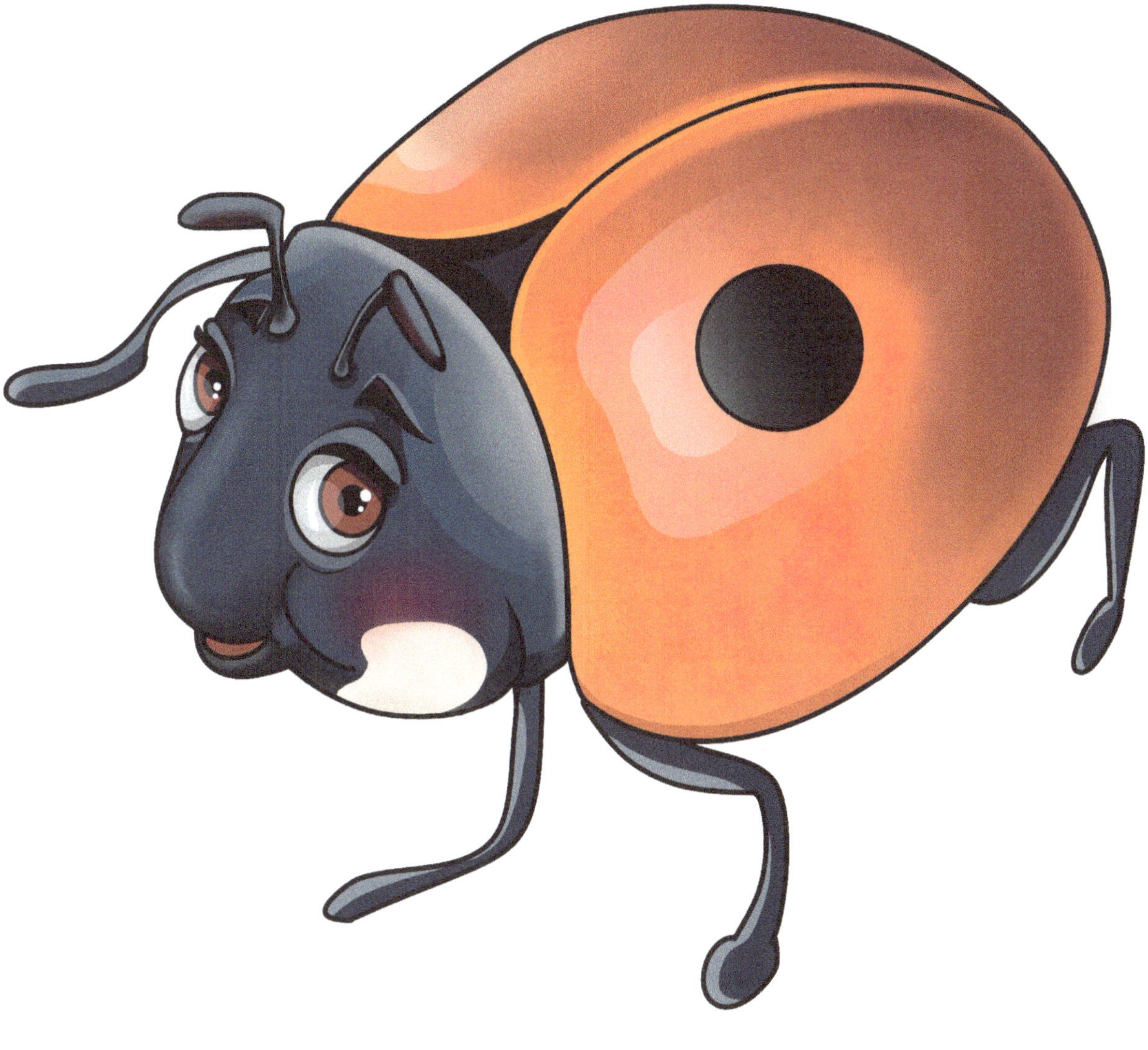

Which one is bigger?

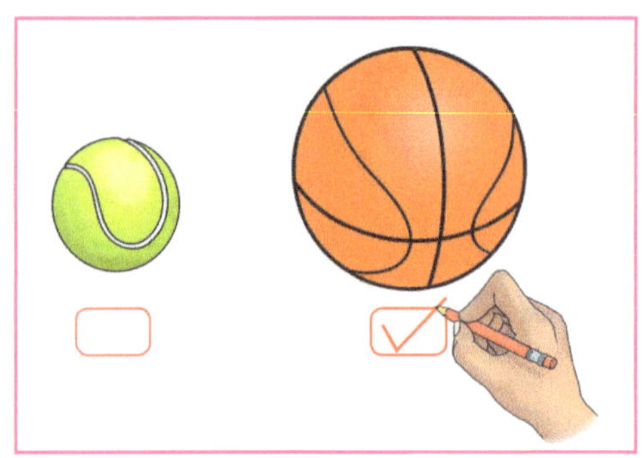

Divide the apple into two equal parts.

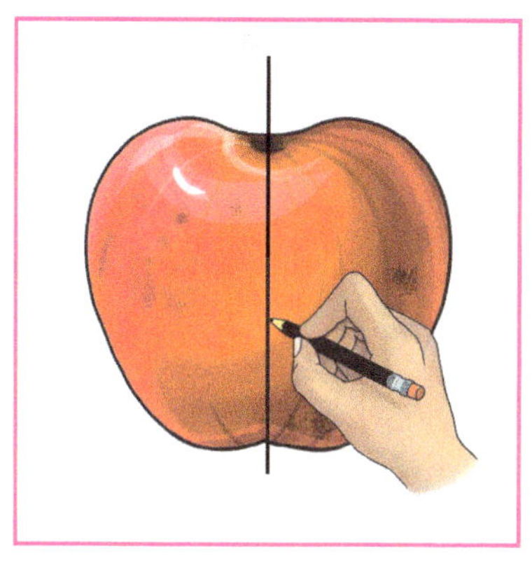

What do we use to catch the fish? Mark it.

Find the objects that are square shaped.

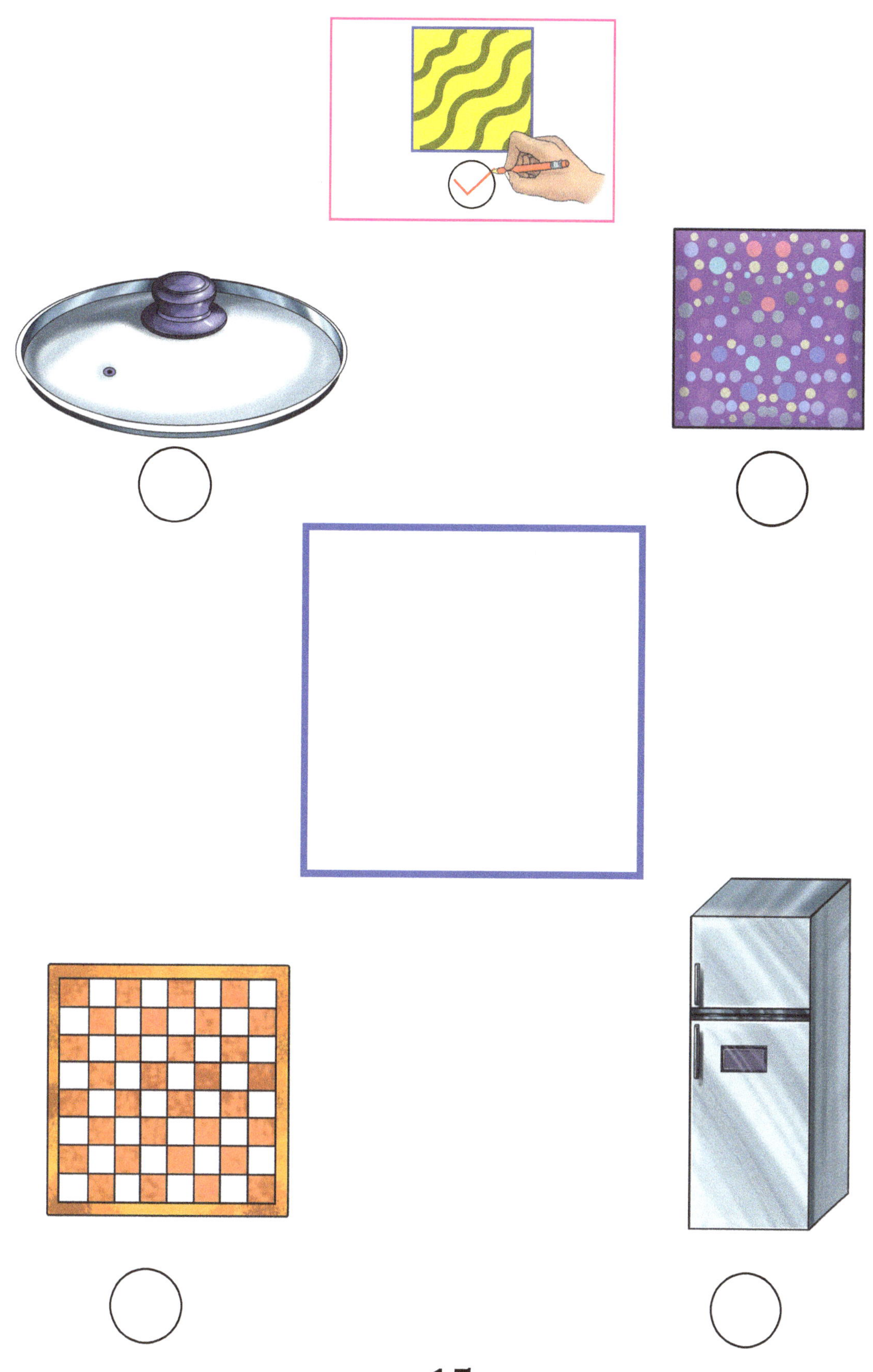

Which symbol does the swan resemble?

Take the bee to the beehive drawing the straight line.

Match the school aids with uncolored shapes.

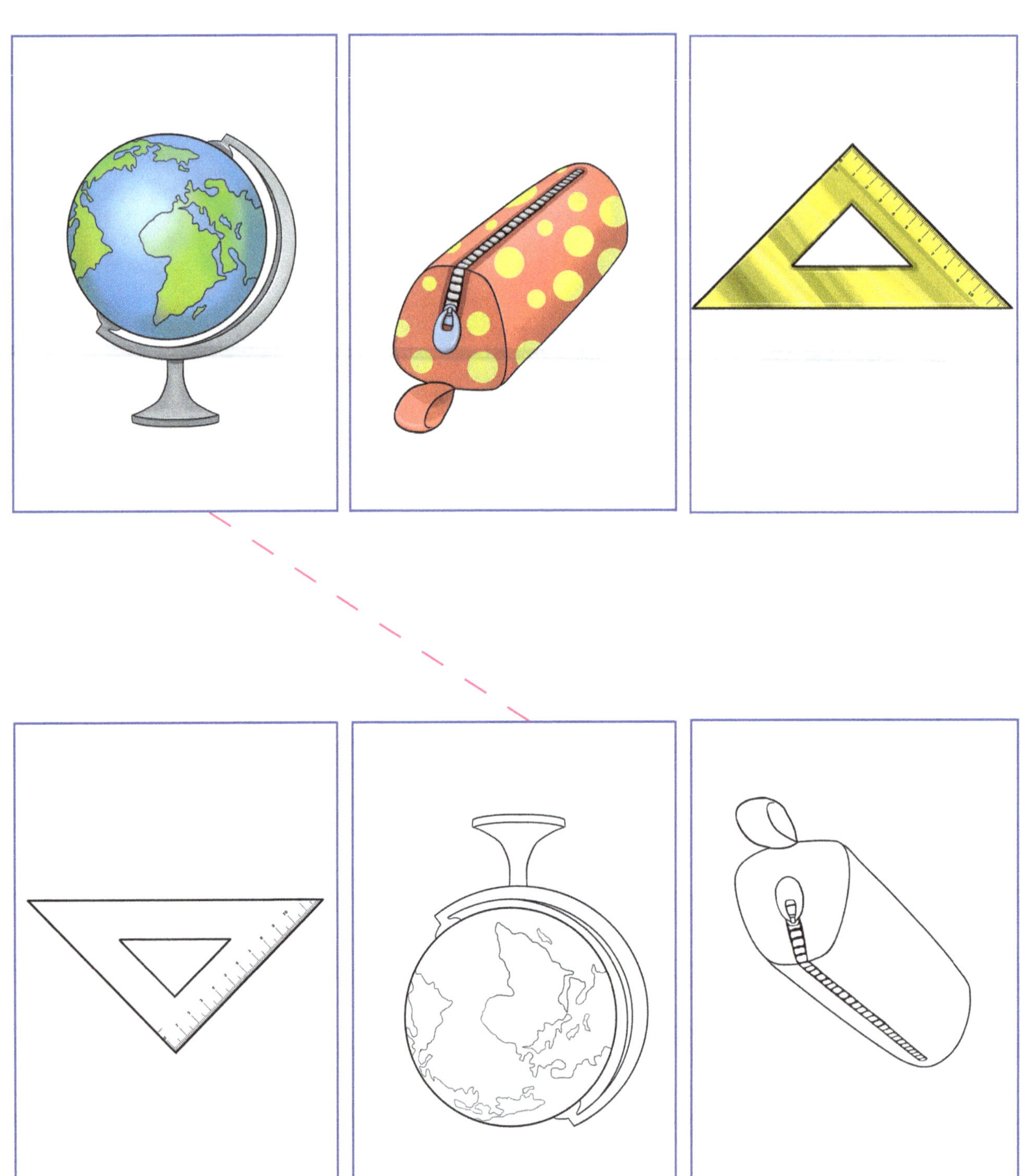

How does the child feel when he receives a present on his birthday? Draw his facial expressions.

Select clothes that are suitable for fall.

Match the black and white shadows of family members.

Match the objects that are in the shadow.

Place heavy and light objects in the appropriate position.

Draw the lines with your both hands at the same time.

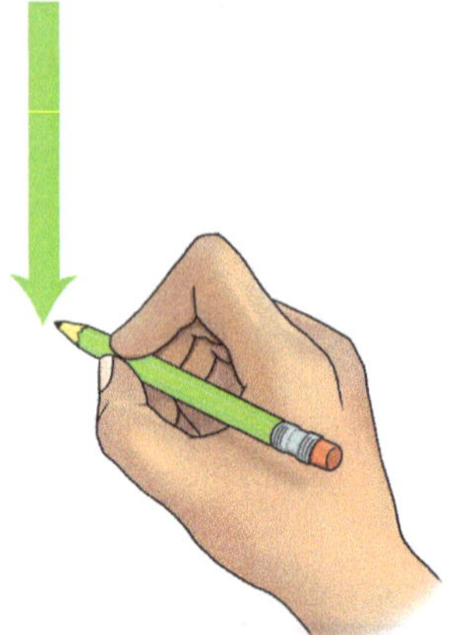

Where does the bear live?

Which one is bitter? Find and mark it.

Do eye exercises following the lines with the baby.
Repeat this exercise at least 5 times.

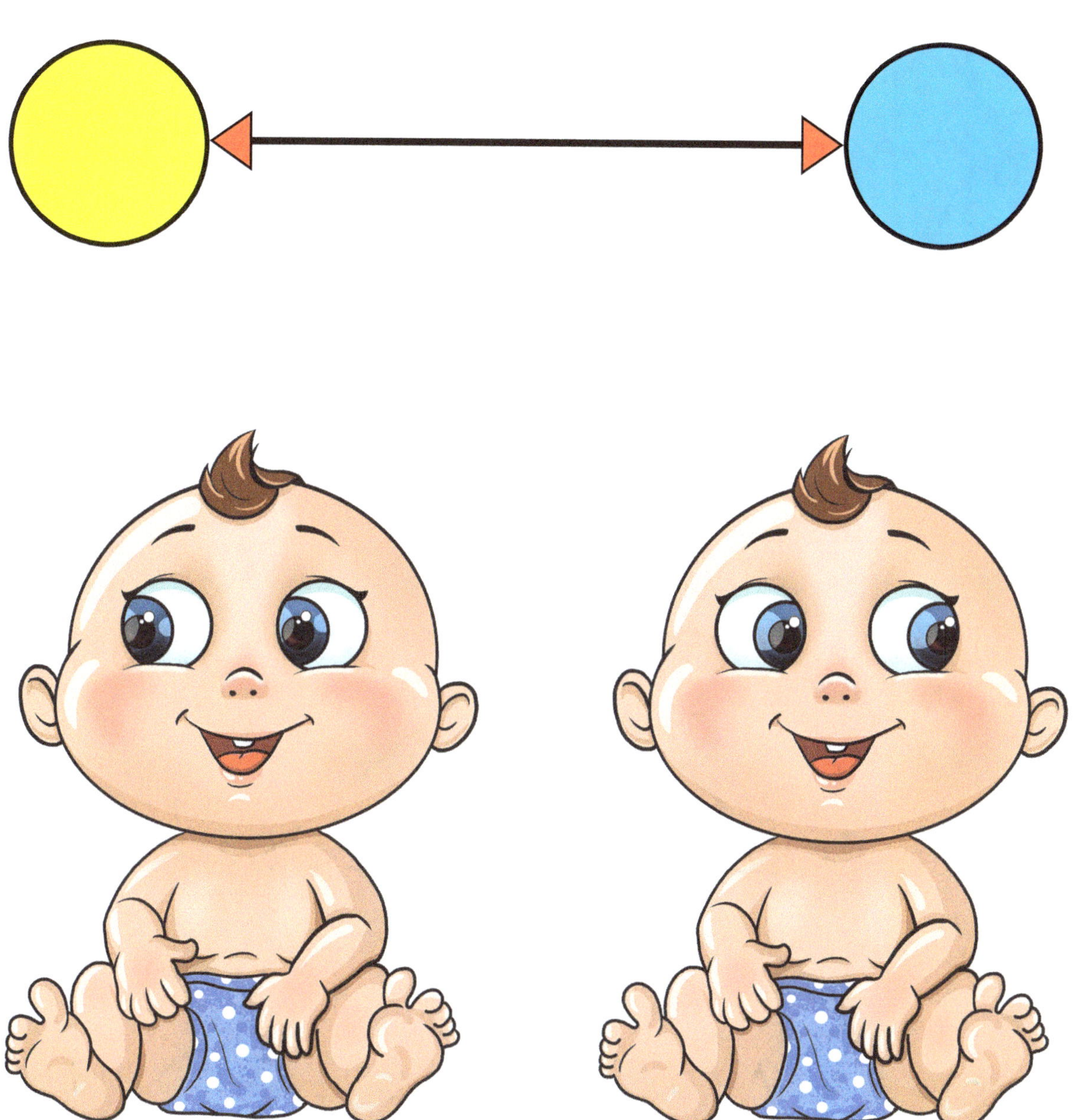

Which geometric figure doesn't fit on the tree below?

Find which symbol is miswritten?

Find the skiing child as in the example in the picture below.

MAGICAL CLOTH

Instruction: Using a cloth as a cover, place a few of the child's toys under the cover. Before uncovering the toys, make a sound that is suitable for the toy. The child is asked which toy he heard the sound of. This game is played in turn with the child.

Suggestion: A large piece of cloth and a few of the boy's toys. In this activity, objects appropriate to the age of the child should be chosen. The game can be continued from easy to difficult.

NO, NO. YES, YES.

Instruction: One of the parents sits with the child. The other parent puts the hat on his feet. The parent and child react and say «no, no». The other parent puts the hat on his head and the mother and child confirm and say «Yes, yes». This game is played in order.
Suggestion: A few clothes are prepared in advance, such as socks, hats and gloves. at least three people have to participate in this game.

9 7 9 8 8 6 9 0 0 6 6 9 1